A Discourse Upon Christian Perfection. By
Mr. de Fenelon, Archbishop of Cambray

A

DISCOURSE

UPON

CHRISTIAN PERFECTION.

By Mr De FENELON,
Archbishop of CAMBRAY.

DUBLIN

Printed for WILLIAM WATSON, Bookseller, at the
Poets Head in Caple-street.

MDCCLIX.

A

DISCOURSE

UPON

CHRISTIAN PERFECTION.

ALL Men muſt make an exact Enqury, into their paſt Lives, becauſe all are Sinners, and ſuch muſt humble themſelves for what is paſt, and be on their Guard for the future

Even thoſe who profeſs Piety, and live exempt from groſs Crimes, muſt examine attentively before God, the Imperfection and little Solidity of their Virtues Without this Examination which preſerves us in Humility, Fear, and diſtruſt of ourſelves, even our Virtues may become Snares or at leaſt prove to us extremely dangerous, by inſpiring us with preſumptuous Confidence, they make us pleaſed with ourſelves, ſo that we paſs our Lives in a State of Illuſion, how many do we ſee, who upon a vain Confidence of their good Intentions, enter upon unwarrantable Conducts? People who are ſo groſsly miſtaken in themſelves that they give Scandal, and ſhock their Neighbours, whilſt they imagine that

A 2 they

they pleafe and edify them, nothing fo fit as fuch
Examples to make us enter into ourfelves, and en
q ire what we are, perhaps we are like thefe de-
ceived People, perhap others look on us with the fame
contemptuous Pity. Thefe People have a good Inten-
tion, and believe their Conduct upright, as we think
ours, are we not in Error? Do we not flatter ourfelves as they do? It is Self-Love which flatters them,
and have not we the fame Seducer within us?

Let us then examine our Paths, the Entrance of
which may be fmooth, and the End of them Death.
We owe fuch Love to God, that our Devotion fhou'd
become Irreprehenfible, as fuch Numbers di-
figure it by their Weaknefs and Indifcretion, we
fhould endeavour to retrieve it's Honour by a different Conduct. What do we not owe to Piety?
Which hath delivered us from an infinite Number
of Errors, that hath conquered our Paffions and Habits, and given us a Difguft to the poifored Pleafures of the World, which hath touched us, and
convinced us of the falutary Truths of Religion,
and which hath protected us from the cunning Snares
of Satan.

And fhall we be ungrateful for thefe Benefits?
Shall not every one of us give up his favourite Inclination in fpite of Self Love, and adorn the Doc-
trines of God our Saviour with all Wifdom. Of all
Things we muft beware of judging of our Virtues
by Appearances: The deceitful Ballances of the
World, which the Scripture calleth abominable, are
entirely different from thofe with which God weigheth
our Actions. God who fearcheth Hearts, often finds
difguifed Paffions in them which he condemneth, tho'
the Outfide appeareth virtuous and exemplary in the
Eyes of the World. Now it is certain, that God
regardeth not the Outfide, that a fuperficial Virtue
can never dazzle him, let us then never be content
or dazzled by it, but examine ourfelves, and try
whether what is effential to Piety be in our
Sentiments and Actions? Whether our Piety is ufe-
ful

ful and unaffected, constant and disinterested? Whether it doth good and concealeth it? Whether it doth not endeavour to please Men, or at least defireth it no farther than it is pleasing to God

A Piety in short which maketh us forget ourselves, excepting when we are to correct our Faults, or perform our Duty once more, let us make this Examination in the Presence of God, and see whether our Piety be of this kind, and let us examine it in Relation to God, ourselves and our Neighbours Every one of us should examine himself whether he be in the Disposition which he ought to be in Relation to God, and without which all his Piety, how soever it ... ...

Do we live to suffer for God?

Are we willing to die to be united to him?

Are we pleased to think of him?

And lastly, are we determined to abandon ourselves to his Conduct?

It is by examining ourselves in these four Particulars, that we shall discover the true State of our Hearts

First, do we love to suffer for God? I do not mean a Sort of vague Love of Sufferings which sheweth itself in Words, and which faileth in Actions, a Love of Suffering which consisteth only in an Habit of Talking magnificently and affectionately of the Excellency and Price of Crosses, whilst we fly them with Delicacy and seek for every Thing that can render Life soft and sensual. Once more, I do not speak of that imaginary Spirituality which maketh us talk of nothing but Resignation, Patience, Joy in Tribulation, whilst we are sensible to the least Inconvenience, and by our whole Conduct testify that we will never suffer any Thing from any One, or want for any Thing we can get

St *Paul* had very different Sentiments from such Christians, when he said he found himself filled with all manner of Joy and Consolation when his Body

A 3   enjoyed

enjoyed no reſt, and that he experienced the rudeſt Tribulations, Combats from without, Fears from within We muſt not imagine that the Zeal of this great Apoſtle need not be imitated by us, under Pretence that the Souls of our Days are leſs ſtrong, leſs elevated To you it is given (as a Favour) ſaith the Apoſtle, not only to believe on him, but alſo to ſuffer for him He makes here no Exceptions of Place and Age Content not yourſelves then, with offering a barren Faith to God, offer him an humble Heart, willing to ſuffer for him, in vain do you follow *Jeſus Chriſt* if you bear not his Croſs, he ſaith himſelf, *whoſoever will be my Servant, he muſt take up his Croſs daily, and follow me*, (without Exception) if we hope to reign with him we muſt ſuffer with him Theſe two States have a neceſſary Connexion, it is the Road he trod, he left us no other, and dare you complain of a Law founded on ſuch an Example? If you ſuffer for *Jeſus Chriſt*, you ſuffer to imitate and pleaſe him, to merit the Joy which he hath promiſed to thoſe who Weep The Hopes of a Chriſtian is to ſuffer here, and be happy hereafter, the falſe Goods of this Life are made for thoſe who hope for, or ſeek no other, the Evils of Life are deſtined by the Mercy of God to elect Souls, whom he will looſen from this World, which is ſo corrupt, and ſo prepare them for Immenſity of Happineſs, in endleſs Duration To ſeek for Happineſs here, is to forget our Exile, to renounce the Hopes of our Country St *Cyprian* told all Chriſtians that in taking the venerable Name of Chriſtian, they devoted themſelves to all Sorts of Sufferings preſent, and ſenſible, in Expectation of an inviſible and eternal Good, that the Heirs of a crucified Saviour, were not permitted to fear either Pains, or Death. Theſe are Truths that we often repeat to others, but do we ſay them to ourſelves? Let us ſincerely compare the Sentiments of our Hearts, with the Principles of the Religion we profeſs, were I thoroughly convinced, that a Chriſtian Life is a Life of Patience, and of continually renouncing my own Inclinations, did I love *Jeſus Chriſt* for humbling himſelf and ſuffering for

me,

me, should I not humble myself and love to suffer for him, in a Time of Danger should I content myself with only talking of Crosses? Should I give Lessons on this Subject to others, and not apply them to myself?

Should I be so impatient under the least Infirmity, so discouraged at the cross Accidents of Life, so uneasy in its Wants and Humors? So delicate and sensible in the Misreckonings upon human Friendship, so jealous, so suspicious so apt to disagree with those I ought to manage, so severe in correcting the Faults of others? So gentle and unmortified when I should mortify my own?

Should I be so sudden and hasty in my Anger, when despised and contradicted, which are all so many Crosses that God lays upon me, to sanctify me by them? Is it not scandalous in those who profess themselves followers of *Jesu Christ* crucified, that they should however by their Delicacy, be the irreconcilable Enemies to the Cross, as St *Paul* expresseth it?

We cannot separate *Christ* and the Cross on which he was crucified for us, and by which he hath drawn us forever to himself.

When will that too just Reproach cease, that Churchmen are too indulgent, too luxurious, too fond of Preferment, and careless of Souls, that Mortification and Self-denial is scarce mentioned by them, much less practised, and yet there is no true Devotion without these.

They object to us, that we will serve God with every Convenience, sigh after the other Life, enjoying all the Sweetness of this, and whilst we declare against Self-love, take all Sorts of Precautions not to mortify it in any Instance in ourselves.

The second Point, is, are we disposed to die, to be united to *Jesus Christ?* St *Paul*, who formed this noble Wish, was desirous that Christians filled with the Hopes of Immortality, should sigh to be delivered from the Weight of their mortal Bodies, and St *Augustine* explaining this Truth in its full Extent, saith, *That Holiness of Life and love of Death, are inseparable*

able

able Dispositions, the Love of these two Lives combat in each other in imperfect Souls. The Love of this passing World is so violent in them, that they possess it with Pleasure, and lose it with Regret The Perfection on the contrary, of Souls very faithful to God, is, that they support Life with Patience, and leave it with Joy, continually longing to go to their blessed Inheritance, to which all things here below appear vile and mean

Let none pretend, saith St *Augustine, that they only desire to live, in order to grow more virtuous* The Truth is, that they are not virtuous enough to wish to Die Not being willing to die, does not proceed from aspiring to an higher Degree of Virtue, but from having obtained but a low One Neither let us alledge the Fear of God s Judgments to justify that of Death, if we only feared the Judgments of God in our Passage to Eternity, this Fear inspired by the *Holy Ghost,* would be moderate, peaceable, and religious, the Perfection of our Love to God, saith St *John, consisteth in our having Confidence in his Day of Judgment, for perfect Love casteth out Fear* If we love him as our Father, should we fear him as our Judge, even so as to fly his Presence ? Should we have those base Fears which trouble, which deject us! Those vain Alarms that we feel, when the Lord knocketh at the Door, and by Sickness telleth that Death is near We weep for the Death of those we love, and fear our own, as if we had no Hope To observe the vain Projects that we make to lengthen Life, and make it agreeable, who would believe that we expect another happy and eternal Life, which this short and miserable one only serveth to retard It is not surprising, that those who confine their Hopes to this Life, fear the End of it; Death is a real Misfortune to such as would not be united to *Jesus Christ,* and who do not hope to reign with him in Eternity ; but for those to whom Religion hath shewed a new and assured Way, to enter into a new Life, and whose Hopes are full of Immortality, can they reconcile these high and solid Hopes with Fear, and a constant Pursuit of trifling Amusements, which stop
their

their Progress in Virtue, and keep them here below by
Inclination? We may conclude, that our Faith and
Piety are very weak and languishing when they cannot overcome the Fear of Death. We must needs see
in a very confused Manner the great Privileges, Hopes,
and Promises of Christianity, not to desire to end Mi-
sery, and begin Happiness. This is precisely then,
what each of us must examine himself upon.

Am I prepared to Die?

Were I to die presently, should I not regret any of
the Creature which surround me? Is there not some-
thing which I thought different to me, that however
I cannot leave without Pain? Am I not blinded so far
as to hug my Chains and love my Slavery? I must
not deceive myself by a false Courage, is it true, that
my Love to *Jesus Christ* overcomes my Fear, and natural Aversion to Death?

Do I use this World as if I used it not? Am I impatient to be no longer subject to its Vanities? is there
nothing allowed by me which prevents these Desires,
and flatters Self-love? Do I not endeavour to render
my Life sweet and agreeable by the Amusements of
Life which I reckon innocent, but which, however,
form in my Heart Attachments contrary to the
Designs of God for me? And am I willing to break
these Chains?

In short, do I prepare myself seriously for Death?
Is it upon this Meditation that I regulate each particular Action of my Life?

When Death arrives with its Rigours, Pains, and
Weakness, shall I be prepared to receive the fatal Blow
with Constancy? What will become of my Fortitude
in these last Moments when I shall find myself betwixt two Worlds, this vanishing from my Sight forever, and Eternity opening itself to receive me? The
Hopes of seeing *Jesus Christ*, that Object of all others
the most amiable, and delightful, should certainly
comfort us against Death, tho' hideous to Nature.

Yet how doth it happen, that People professing
Piety, often fear it as much as others? That the least
Infirmity alarms and dejects them, and one may ob-

A 5   serve

ferve as much anxious Care and Delicacy for their Pre-
fervation, as in worldly People, must we not confess,
that this is shameful ? In vain do we prepare for
Death by a retired and pious Life, if this Preparation
only ends in being furprized and troubled at whatever
Hour that Death may arrive

Are we delighted to think of God ? That is to fay,
do we feel a fincere Joy when we Pray to him, when
we meditate in his Prefence on the Truths of Religion,
Prayer is the Meafure of Love, as we are more fervent in Prayer, we are more elevated in divine Love

    Who loves much prays much,

    Who loves little prays little

He whofe Heart is ftrictly united to God, has not fo
high a Pleafure as that of never lofing his Prefence
He feels a fenfible Delight in fpeaking to God, think-
ing of his eternal Truths, adoring his Goodnefs, ad
miring his Works, praifing his Mercy, charmed with
his Power and Wifdom, abandoning Himfelf to his
Providence, in this Commerce of the Creature with
God, it unbofoms its Cares, Fears, Anxieties, to the
tendereft of Fathers, and it receives eafe by opening its
Heart to its moft faithful Friend, it fhews with Confidence its Weakneffes and ever finds God a Refource
in all Evils, a Shelter from all Adverfity As we are
imperfect during Life, never exempt from Sin, all the
Life of a Chriftian muft pafs in Penitence for our Faults,
and Thankfulnefs to God for his Goodnefs, and it is
in the Exercife of Prayer that we can afk Pardon of
God for our Ingratitude, and thank him for his Mercy.
Piety is never perfected in us but by Fidelity in Prayer
God will make us feel by Experience, that we can
only obtain his Love from him, that this Love which
alone is Religion, and the only Happinefs of our Souls,
can neither be acquired by the Reflections of our Un-
derftandings, nor the natural Efforts of our Hearts,
only by *the gratuitous Effufion of the Holy Ghoft*

This Love is fuch a Gift, that God alone will give
it, but it muft be to thofe who afk it, thus we muft by
a faithful and conftant Application to God earneftly beg
this Love that we may obtain it.

                       We

We may blame ourselves if our Piety hath not that Solidity and Confidence which is certainly produced by a good Prayer, for without this Exercise, by which we imprint strongly in our Minds and Hearts, all the Truths of Religion, by which we accustom ourselves happily to taste and follow them; all the Sentiments of Piety which pass thro' the Mind unattended to, are only transient Fervors that pass away. Let us Pray then, but always with a View to our Duties, let us not Pray to be more enlightened and spiritual in Words, but to become more humble, more teachable, more patient, more charitable, more modest, more pure, and more disinterested in every Instance of our Conduct, without this, our Assiduity in Prayer very far from being fruitful and efficacious, will be full of Illusion for us, and Scandal for our Neighbour. Of Illusion to us; how many Examples have we of People whose Prayers only nourish their Pride, and mislead their Imaginations? Of Scandal to our Neighbour. For is there any Thing more scandalous than to see a Person who prays constantly without correcting his Faults, who comes from Prayers as uneasy, chagrined, angry, proud, and irritated as he was before he prayed.

Are we are determined to abandon ourselves to God with Confidence? Do we depend upon his Providence as our best Resource? Or have we not rather a political Providence that is timorous and uneasy, which in his is unworthy of the Assistance of the Providence of God?

The Generality of those who would give themselves to God, are like the young Gentleman in the Gospel, they have some Reserve, and that Reserve prevents their Perfection, and prevents their being accepted of by God, they would both fain serve God and Mammon, but they cannot serve two Masters.

The essential Disposition of a Heart devoted to God, is to depend on him for every Thing, using the Means he hath ordained for the obtaining of them, and after having done so, rest assured that God is Master of all Events.

We

We muft each Moment fuppreſs the covetouſneſs of Nature, which inceſſantly fears the Loſs of what it poſſeſſeth, and deſireth the Poſſeſſion of what it hath not. We muſt deſire nothing, will nothing, which may trouble or diſturb the Deſigns of God for us.

We muſt be continually upon our Guard againſt Self-Love, which inceſſantly endeavours to make us amends by the Amuſement of little Things for the Sacrifice of greater, which we have made to God. For can there be any Thing more deplorable, than to ſee People, who after having taken the firſt Steps towards Perfection, look back, and apprehend that they ſhall do too much?

However, can we ſay that many Souls are exempt from this Baſeneſs?

Is it not true, that this Gift of ourſelves to God, by our Manner of ſerving him, reduces this Gift and Service almoſt to nothing?

We almoſt make our ſpiritual Intereſts give Place to our temporal Ones, we would accompliſh our Duties and ſatisfy our Conſciences, but we will do this with ſo many Conditions, we are ſo fearful, ſo cautious, leſt we ſhould do or ſuffer too much to pleaſe God, that in Effect, we do little or nothing, we foreſee ſo many Inconveniencies, we will aſſure ourſelves of ſo many Conſolations and Aſſiſtances, that inſenſibly we reduce the Practice of Chriſtianity to the Faſhions of the World, by our languiſhing timorous Performance of it's Duties. Why do ſo many undertake good Works without Succeſs? Becauſe they do not renounce themſelves in theſe Undertakings. Such timorous diſcreet Worldling, have not the Generoſity and Force which are neceſſary to uphold the Deſigns of God. No, God will diſdain to bleſs theſe Conducts which are too human from ſuch proceed Lukewarmneſs, and a miſerable Diſcharge of all Duties. God pours his Riches with divine Profuſion, but it is upon thoſe Perſons who invoke him, who will truſt in none but him, and not to ſuch as will prevent his Providence, and never be reduced to truſt to it.

Is

It is Time to confider our Difpofitions in regard to ourfelves

Let us examine ourfelves, whether our Zeal be not imprudent, under the Cloak of Religion?

Whether our Prudence be not worldly Policy?

Whether our Devotion be not the Effects of our Humour

Whether our Charity is not an Amufement? Here are four Queftions which we fhould put to ourfelves

Firft, is not our Zeal imprudent? Let all Roots of Bitternefs be deftroyed in you, faid St *Paul*, there is a bitter Zeal which muft be corrected, to hear it, all muft inftantly fubmit to its Cenfures, all muft be rigorouſly judged by it, but obferve the Original of this pretended Zeal, it is becaufe our Neighbour's Faults fhock our, our Vanity cannot bear another's Vanity Our Haughtinefs makes their Pride infupportable, our Reftlefinefs detefts their Sloth, our Spleen their Amufements, our Interetftednefs, their Cunning and Addrefs to cheat us. Were we Faultlefs, we fhould lefs feel the Defects of thofe we are obliged to live with, it is even certain, that this Contrariety and Sort of Combat betwixt our Faults and our Neighbours, encreafes the lift extremely in our Imagination already prejudiced. Now, can we difcover a more malignant Source than this cenforious Zeal proceeds from?

Did we own fincerely, that we have not Virtue enough to fupport patiently the Want of it in our Neighbour, we fhould feem weak ourfelves, and that Vanity forbids, on the contrary, it muft needs change our Faults into Virtues, Weaknefs muft be Force, Pride, Zeal, indeed, an imaginary and often an hypocritical Zeal For, is it not admirable to obferve how quiet and indifferent we are to thofe Faults in others which give us no Trouble, whilft this fire Zeal is kindled in us, againft thofe who raife our Jealoufy, tire our Patience, or thwart our Interefts A convenient Zeal this, which is only exerted for ourfelves, we wifh to Rife by the Faults of others. Were our Zeal a Chriftian one, it would begin at Home, and we fhould be fo much taken up with our own Defects,

Miferies,

Miseries and Faults, that we should scarce have Time (even from Charity) to think of those of others If we could prevail on ourselves to do so, it must proceed from an Obligation of Conscience thus to inspect the Conduct of our Neighbour, even when we were indispensibly bound to watch over him, and even in that Case, we should act with great Precaution for ourselves, according to the Advice of the Apostle, *Gal* vi 1 *Correct thy Brother with Gentleness, lest thou shouldest be tempted, whilst thou art helping him out of Temptation* In correcting his ill Humour, you run a Risque of following your own, in suppressing his Pride and angry Passions, you may kindle your own Alas ! Beware then, of so zealously providing for the Perfection of your Neighbour, as to forget your own It would be very imprudent Zeal to neglect our own Affairs, and preside over those of others It is true, that the Zeal which animates a Christian for the Correction of his Brother, when it is both pure and prudent, is a Zeal which is highly pleasing to God , but we are not to believe it is disinterested, unless it bears the Marks of the Wisdom from above, which is first pure, then gentle, and always sweet and moderate For the Zeal which kindles against our Neighbour, which will forgive him nothing, which will needs have him think as we do, before he is convinced, and which will torment him if he doth not, such a Zeal is earthly, sensual, devilish, all that is done or said with Warmth, is not fit for the Information, or Correction of our Brother Where do we perceive any good Effects from these hard Conducts ? We must gain Hearts when Religion is in Question, and Hearts are gained by Marks of Love and Condescension. It is not sufficient to have Reason on our Side, we spoil, we dishonour Reason, when we support it with an over-bearing Arrogance. Conviction must be free, it is by Sweetness and Affection that we gain Minds, that we dispose them to listen to Truth, and to suspect their old Opinions , Mens Prejudices must be ript, not torn from them We must first convince them that we love them, and this will inspire them with the necessary Confidence in us

to

to be of Use to them , and encourage them to conquer their former Errors and Habits Self love, never
fails to rife against ill humoured Councils, however j ft
they may be. Even God doth not blefs fuch Conduct,
for the Wrath of Man worketh not his Righteoufnefs.

Is not our Prudence worldly Policy? This fleflhly
Wifdom the Apoftle fays is but Death, for it is not fub-
mitted to the Will of God, and cannot be fo. There
is an abfolute Incompatibility between this Wifdom
from below and the Wifdom from above, it is this
earthy Policy which refifteth the Spirit of God, grieves
it, and traverfes the Defigns which he hath for the
Perfection of our Souls.

This is the Wifdom by which a Chriftian fhuts himfelf up in himfelf, and trufts to his own Light of Reafon entirely, and thereby fruftrateth the greateft of
God's Gifts, GRACE. This earthly, fenfual, devilifh
Wifdom, fo often reproved in the Gofpel, is however
deep rooted in the Hearts of moft Chriftians, how
many human Confiderations do we daily fee fruftrate
the Works of God? How many imaginary fafhionable
Decencies flop the Mouths of Chriftians, when the
moft facred Truths are boldly attacked, thus we bafely
give up to the World what is moft holy and moft
venerable.

Formerly Chriftians were a People who defpifed the
ill founded Contempt of the World, to ferve God
with Liberty. At prefent Chriftians, and even fome of
thofe retired from the World, fear it's Cenfures,
defire it's Approbation, and regulate their Conduct
and Opinions upon certain Prejudices, by which the
World praifes and blames as it pleafeth.

It feems, that this timid Weaknefs was never car-
ried fo far as at prefent, for we regulate by this worldly Prudence, Works which relate to the Glory of
God , and determine how far each particular Perfon
fhould practife Virtue. And from a thoufand Confiderations merely human, dare not undertake for the
Intereft of God, any Thing which is not to the Tafte
of the World.

Yet

Yet we confult the World though a declared Enemy to God, in Relation to the moft holy Matters, we do not confult fo far as not to give juft Offence, which is right, but we confult it to accommodate it's vain Maxims with Chriftian Piety, and make our good Actions depend upon it's Decifions, this worldy Prudence infects moft People. How many vain Defires to gain or keep the Favour of thofe in Authority? How many flattering Cares to gain their Efteem, to be confidered and taken Notice of by them? What Regrets and Uneafinefs when we fail in our Attempts this Way? What Grief when we lofe thefe vain Confolations?

When we ferve God with thefe Referves, we ferve him weakly, we divide our Hearts and our Cares betwixt him and a thoufand Things unworthy to enter into Competition with him, in this Situation God muft wait for Occafions, his Service muft give Way to Times and Seafons, not only he muft wait, but he muft often be refufed. It is true we defire his Glory, we wifh to do good, but we wifh it upon fuch Conditions, as make our good Intentions vanifh, for we can never ferve two Mafters.

We drag along, faith St *Auguftine*, a weak and languifhing Will to the practice of Virtue, which amufes our Minds, without changing our Hearts.

Who amongft us defireth Perfection as he ought to defire it? Who amongft us defires Perfection more than Pleafure, more than Honour? Who amongft us loves Chriftian Perfection fo much, as to facrifice all Amufements which are contrary to it? Let us endeavour from this Moment to regulate our Prudence by the Spirit of God. Let it not be a prefumptuous Prudence accommodated to the Diffimulation of the Age, let us be prudent to do Good, and fo innocent if poffible, as not to know Evil. Let us have that greateft of all Prudence to glorify God, to advance his Intereft, and do Honour to Religion by our Lives, and may we then forget ourfelves, and think we are unprofitable Servants?

Is

Is not our Devotion the Effect of our Humour? The Apostle fore-telling the Dangers which threatened Religion, said, *There should arise vain Men, lovers of themselves*, such are to be seen every Day in all States of Life, even amongst retired Christians, there are People who leave the World and it's Vanities to satisfy a melancholy sour Disposition, others are mild and quiet from Indolence, rather than Virtue, there are Devotions of every Constitution, tho' but one Gospel, and every one adjusts it to his particular Inclinations, whereas Christians should continually resist their Inclinations, to conform to this holy Rule, and not bend it to their Humours. Yet where shall we find this admirable Conformity to all it's Precepts? We see every where Religion disfigured by Peoples Attempts to regulate it to their low Conceptions of it, to their Fancies and Caprices.

One is fervent at Prayer, but hard, severe, and censorious, unable to overlook and pardon the Weaknesses and Follies of others. Another talks well on the Subject of Resignation and Crosses, but cannot bear the least Contradiction or Disappointment. Some will fast and mortify their Bodies, but take no Care to sweeten their Tempers, which remain harsh and insupportable. Some are fervent and pleased with private Devotion, but weary and wandering at publick Worship where their Duty equally calls them. And sometimes when People discharge an important Part of Duty well, they imagine they may be excused from the common Ones which every Hour furnishes them. Is it not deplorable, that some People otherwise good, persuade themselves, because they practise some Virtues which give them Trouble, that this gives them a Title to be troublesome to others, and to flatter themselves in their Predominant Inclinations. It would indeed be better to be gentler both to yourself and others, and not to be so zealous, and troublesome at once, let every Virtue in it's Place, according to your Measure of Grace, and do not pretend to practise them at the Expence of others.

Justice and Charity are the first of all human Virtues. Why should you attach yourself to others in prejudice

judice of thefe ? Or to thefe, in Prejudice of each
other ? As for Inftance, fome People fhould be juft,
before they become generous be ſtrict to yourſelf, but
be humble, be zealous for the Reputation of others,
but be good humoured, charitable polite and courteous
Do all you can for the glory of God, but begin with
the Duties of your Station, without this univerſal
Attention and Obedience to God's Commands,
your Virtues will degenerate into Whims, and your
Example will deter from, and not invite People to
Religion It is the Sign of a great Degree of Grace,
to bear with a ſmall Degree of it in others Why is
Piety decryed by Men of the World ? Becaufe wrong-
headed People reduce it to the Practice of low fuper-
fluous Things, and forfake what is eſſential to it

Is not our Charity an Amuſement ? Are not our
Friendſhips vain and ill chofen ? Is not it true, that we
are oftner faithlefs to God by our Friendſhips, than
from our Enmities, there is ſo terrible a Law which
forbids hating our Neighbour, that when we furprize
ourfelves in Sentiments of Hatred and Revenge, that
Animofity gives us Horror, and we make hafte to be
reconciled to our Brother, but as to our Friendſhips,
it is not the fame, we are convinced that nothing is
fweeter, more innocent and natural, or more conform-
able to Charity than to love our Brethren, even Religion ferves as a Pretence to the Temptation

Thus we are not enough upon our Guard, in relation to our Friendſhips, we form them often without
Choice, and from no Rule but Inclination, or blind
Prejudice, let us give every Thing we love it's proper
Rank in our Hearts, do we love with Preference thofe
we can lead to God, who are fit to lead us to him ? Do
we not feek for vain Pleafures in them ? Alas ! How
much frivolous Amufement in our Friendſhips ? How
much Time loft in teftifying it, and often with little
ſincerity ? How many Heart-openings, and Confiden-
ces, which only ferve to encreafe Pain and excite Com-
plaints ? How many particular Attachments, which prevents more univerfal Love ? How many Preferences
that offend.

I

I know it is permitted to love certain Persons (where Merit diftinguifh them, or to whom Providence hath connected us) with greater Tendernefs than others

But you muft be difcreet even in thefe Friendfhips, they muft be in the Bottom of your Heart, and no more muft appear outwardly than what is neceffary to fhew Efteem, Gratitude, and the Cordiality of Friend-fhip which we owe them, as to affected Cares and Tendernefles, they only excite Jealoufy and give Pain to others Even the holieft Friendfhips muft keep within thefe Bounds (our Duty to our Neighbour) We muft not only examine the Sentiments of our Hearts, but we muft likewife ftudy the Detail of our Actions, in Relation to our Neighbour. As to outward Conduct, we have three Things to do.

To Condefcend,
To Act,
To Suffer

1 To condefcend The Foundation of Peace with all Men is Humility. God refifteth the Proud, and Men through Pride, continually refift each other, thus it is effential to the Succefs of every Undertaking where Men act in Concert, that they fhould humble them-felves Pride is incompatible with Pride, from thence arifeth all the Divifors which trouble the World

And with ftronger Reafon, the Works of God which are all founded in Humility, can only be fupported by the Means which the Son of God chofe himfelf for his great Work, the Eftablifhment of Religion

We muft be fubmiffive to every Creature, faith St *Peter* 1 ch 1 ver. We muft conquer all Sorts of Diffi-culties by a perpetual Patience, and Humility, we muft always be ready to perform the 'oweft, the moft defpicable Functions according to the World, and fear thofe which are elevated, and to which fome Honour and Authority is annexed, we muft fincerely love to be forgotten by the World, in obfcurity, confidering that State as an happy Harbour, and avoiding all Things that may take us out
of

of it, and procure us some Renown, we must renounce from our Hearts all Reputation of Wit, Virtue, or Merit which gives us secret Pleasure, a vile and unworthy Recompence which frustrates those that God would give us, for sacrificing all to him.

In a Word, we must say in an humble Retreat what the inspired King said, when he humbled himself to honour God in his Triumph. *I will still be come more and more vile in my own Eyes, that I may please those of God.*

If we do not love Humility, we shall not subject ourselves to it with Pleasure, if we do not obey with an humble Docility, we obey, though the Greatness and Majesty of the Word, it is not this base kind of concealed Pride, disguised, I say, to others and ourselves, which saps by little and little the Fruits of Religion, and which corrupts by little and little the Fruits of our Virtues. Is it not these presumptuous People who are critical, disdainful, and odd, extreme in their Sentiments? Who, desirous of redressing all Things according to their Views, go astray, and are incapable of accommodating themselves to other Men, to concur with them in the Works of God.

We must stifle in the Bottom of our Hearts all growing Jealousies, all the Traps for Praise and Honour; a vain Desire to please, to succeed to be praised, and the Fear of seeing others preferred to us. We must conquer the Desire to decide, dictate, and act of ourselves, and the natural Passion to govern, and to see our Sentiments prevail over the Sentiments of others.

Since *Jesus Christ* hath entailed Men of all Conditions by calling all Men (according to the Apostle) it followeth, That all those Differences which flatter the Ambition of Men, are ruined by Christianity, when God hath levelled all Men by the Equality of his most precious Gift Faith. It is in vain to pretend to distinguish ourselves by Advantages which are not real, let each forget if it be necessary what they have been, to remember what they are, let the Sons and Daughters of God despise all other Titles; and not despise their Brethren
for

for the want of them, let them neither esteem themselves for natural or acquired Talents, and be foremost
in Deference and Honours, of others, as St *Paul* said,
Be courteous to all Men, honour all Men These Rules
are easily given, but we cannot obey them with the
same Facility Nature must first be well destroyed by
Grace in our Hearts, to be able constantly in every
Particular to observe so perfect a Conduct, and so
numble

Not only Pride, but even Spirit and Delicacy, natural to certain Minds, renders such Conduct extremely difficult, for instead of respecting their Neighbour
with a true Sentiment of Humility, all their Charity
consists in enduring them with a Compassion very like
Contempt, you see there is much to be done in the best
of us, it is necessary to use the utmost Diligence whilst
Time so short and precious is given to us Life is short,
let us make haste to employ it, let every Moment of it be
consecrated to good Works. For when every Thing else
shall vanish forever from us, *the Works of the Just will
be their faithful Companions beyond the Grave, they shall
follow them,* saith the *Holy Ghost,* Rev xiv 13
Besides, it is certain, as St *Paul* finely expresseth it,
That we were created in Jesus Christ *for good Works,
that we should walk in them* That is to say, according
to the Language of Scripture, *To pass all our Life
in this happy Application* Let us then do Good according to the Power which God hath given us, in the
State of Life in which he hath placed us Let us do
Good,

> *With Discernment,*
> *With Courage,*
> *With Perseverance.*

The Love which is called Charity, only acteth to
increase God's Glory, it can stop for that Reason when
Discretion requireth it, it will not engage inconsiderately
in disproportioned Designs.

With

With Courage, for St *Paul* exhorteth us in *Gal.
Not to fail whilst we are doing Good thro' want of
Zeal and Faith.*

With Perseverance Because we often see light,
easy, and inconstant Minds look back too soon,
we shall every where find Opportunities of doing
Good, they present themselves to us continually,
and almost every where, the Will to perform them
fails us It is true, that we must act discreetly with
Precaution and Counsel, lest, that whilst we are intent
upon the Sanctification of others, we should work in
sensibly to our own Reprobation But however, let us
not be like some devout People, who only think of
themselves, who retrench their Care and Attention to
their own Safety, and are insensible to that of others,
Charity tho' prudent, is disinterested, and when
God deigns to make use of us, when he trusts (upon
some Occasions) the Interests of his Glory to our Care,
do you apprehend that he will forget yours?

Lastly, We must suffer

I finish this Discourse with one of the principal
Truths which I explained from the Beginning Yes, it
is necessary to suffer, not only to submit ourselves to
Providence, in order to expiate our Faults, and to
sanctify us by the Virtues of Affliction, but it is likewise often necessary that we should suffer, to make the
Works of God succeed which are intrusted to us, the
Apostles, according to the Picture which the great
Apostle himself gives of them, were Men who gave
themselves up to all Sorts of Injuries, Wrongs, and
Torments, for preaching the Gospel Some envious and
artificial People preached the Gospel, in order to raise
a more cruel Persecution to St. *Paul,* and to render his
Captivity and Bonds more rude, no Matter, said he,
provided that their Malice and my Patience in thy La-
bour, make *Jesus Christ* known, these are the Sentiments that we should have for the Designs of God, to
which he maketh us instrumental, when their Success
dependeth on our Sufferings, let us suffer with Joy?
Happy when God makes his Cause ours, and when for
his Glory, we suffer for his Glory Likewise will he
himself

himself comfort us, and wipe all Tears from our Eyes
Whosoever will serve God, must suffer Persecution, St.
Paul saith, and the Wise Men said, ' My Son, by
' engaging yourself in the happy Service of God,
' you must prepare yourself for Temptations Pro-
' vide yourself with Courage and Patience, you will
' suffer Tribulations and Traverses, which will shake
' your Constancy, if your Faith and Charity have not
' a strong Foundation, the World will blame, will
' tempt you, and will not permit you to enjoy even
' your Retirement in Peace, your Friends and your
' Enemies will act in Concert to ruin you, at least to
' frustrate your pious Designs, even those with whom
' you are united to glorify God, will lay in your Way
' a Sort of Temptation, from an Opposition of Hu-
' mours and Sentiments, different Views and Customs,
' these Things will make you suffer much from those
' you looked upon as your Support, and Consolation,
' their Faults and yours will perpetually shock each
' other, because you will be every Hour together, if
' Charity doth not sweeten your Pains, if more than a
' moderate Degree of Virtue doth not remove the
' Bitterness of your State, if constant Fervour in
' Prayer doth not lighten the Yoke of the Lord, it
' will grow so heavy that you will sink under it In
' these Circumstances you will be so taken up with your
' own Uneasiness, that instead of working in Union
' with other Labourers in the common Work, that
' you will be reduced to seek, to beg, every Hour
' for Counsel and Consolation, to support your
' Weakness in the midst of such Disgusts, and far from
' advancing the Glory of God, all that you will be
' able to do, will be to keep yourself from being
' hurt, and to avoid the giving of Scandal by your
' Divisions' This is but too faithful a Picture of
the Dangers we are in I am not ignorant of the
Graces which God will give, but I remind you,
that the more you have received of the Gifts of
God, the more you should fear being unfaithful
to him It is you who are to give as much Glory

and

and Joy to his Church, as bad Chriſtians cauſe Shame and Grief to it, 'tis you who are to comfort her by your Virtue, and to aſſiſt even her worſt and moſt erroneous Children By your Prayers, Example, and Care, God grant that you may ever riſe from Virtue to Virtue, and that being the moſt illuſtrious Part of *Jeſus Chriſt's* Flock, you may be one with him, as he is with his Father to all Eternity *Amen*

The END.